WALTER JOHNSON

NLP Techniques

Your Easy Guide To Understand How NLP Works, Its Importance And Effectiveness To Learn NLP Components And Techniques To Become The Master Of Your Success

Copyright © 2021 Walter Johnson

All rights reserved.

© **Copyright 2021 - All rights reserved.**

The content contained within this book may not be reproduced, duplicated or transmitted without direct written permission from the author or the publisher.

Under no circumstances will any blame or legal responsibility be held against the publisher, or author, for any damages, reparation, or monetary loss due to the information contained within this book. Either directly or indirectly.

Legal Notice:

This book is copyright protected. This book is only for personal use. You cannot amend, distribute, sell, use, quote or paraphrase any part, or the content within this book, without the consent of the author or publisher.

Disclaimer Notice:

Please note the information contained within this document is for educational and entertainment purposes only. All effort has been executed to present accurate, up to date, and reliable, complete information. No warranties of any kind are declared or implied. Readers acknowledge that the author is not engaging in the rendering of legal, financial, medical or professional advice. The content within this book has been derived from various sources. Please consult a licensed professional before attempting any techniques outlined in this book.

By reading this document, the reader agrees that under no circumstances is the author responsible for any losses, direct or indirect, which are incurred as a result of the use of information contained within this document, including, but not limited to, — errors, omissions, or inaccuracies.

Introduction 5

Chapter 1. Neuro-Linguistic Programming (NLP) 10

Chapter 2. How NLP Works, Importance of NLP, and is NLP Effective? 17

Chapter 3. Components of NLP and NLP Techniques 23

Chapter 4. The Swish Pattern 28

Chapter 5. Hypnosis 35

Chapter 6. Brainwashing 41

Chapter 7. How to Use NLP for in Sales 46

Chapter 8. How to Use NLP in Relationships 49

Chapter 9. NLP in Business 55

Chapter 10. Body Language and Behavior Imitation 62

Chapter 11. Using NLP to Manage People 68

Conclusion 74

Introduction

NLP refers to the ability to sway interactions with other people. It has several different stages when used, beginning with establishing rapport and ending in getting the desired result. Ultimately, it is guided by non-verbal responses and reactions of the client, which can be used first to create rapport and sway the other person to do what is necessary.

NLP starts with developing rapport, which is typically done through mirroring and matching behaviors. You can cue the other person to begin identifying more with you when you use mirroring first. Following the other person's behaviors as a guide in interacting with him or her, you can begin keying into their desire to like you. They are more likely to identify with and trust you if you are mirroring them. It opens them up to the following step.

You will then be gathering information about the other person's mental state. It is using a study of body language or the way the other person may answer. When you understand the other person's mental state, you can begin understanding what their thought processes are, as well as the wording they use. It is where you start to understand the linguistic and programming parts of NLP. You can understand the other person's mind through understanding their words. You can begin to understand the mindset based on the wording, such as focusing on sensory-based metaphors or focusing on certain tendencies. You understand their programming by watching their body language with their words.

From there, it is time to start coming in on changing their minds. When the other person readily mirrors your interactions, you can begin speaking to the other person and mirroring the behaviors you want. For example, if you wish the other person to be more comfortable with spiders, you make a subtle body language sign that you are comfortable with when you mention spiders. You may learn in a little bit toward the other person, conveying that you are comfortable as you mention the spider. The other person should mirror your response, and as they do so, they tell their minds that there is nothing to fear, nothing to worry about, and that everything is fine.

This sort of process can then be expanded upon to be used for everything from depression to creating self-confidence in another person. It is, essentially, swaying the other person to feel more comfortable with things that may have been uncomfortable before. It allows you to sway opinions, behavior, goals, and more just by tuning into their body language, ensuring that you share rapport, and using that rapport to slowly mold the other person's mind to mimic the one you are attempting to create.

Historically, persuasion is rooted in ancient Greek's model of a prized politician and orator.

To make a list, a politician or speaker needs to master rhetoric and elocution to persuade the public. Rhetoric, according to Aristotle, is the "ability to make use of the available methods of persuasion" to win a court case or influence the public during important orations. On the other hand, elocution (a branch of rhetoric) is the art of speech delivery, including proper diction, proper gestures, stance, and dress. Although Grecian politics and orations seem clearly to be the genesis of persuasion, its use in the rapidly developing world of the twenty-first century goes beyond politics, oration, and other human endeavors.

In the business domain, persuasion refers to a corporate system of influence to change other people, groups, or organizations' attitudes, behavior, or perception about an idea, object, goods, services, or people. It often employs verbal communications (both written and spoken words), non-verbal communication (paralinguistic, chronemics, proxemics, and so on), visual communication, or multimodal communication to convey, change or reinforce a piece of existing information or reasoning peculiar to the audience. Persuasion in business can come in different forms depending on the need of the management. For instance, business enterprise sometimes uses persuasion in cases like; public relations, broadcast, media relations, speech writing, social media, client relations, employee communication, brand management, etc.

In psychological parlance, persuasion refers to using an obtainable understanding of the social, behavioral, or cognitive principles in psychology to influence the attitude, cognition, behavior, or belief system of a person, group, or organization. It is also seen as a process by which a person's attitude and behavior are influenced without coercion but through the simple means of communication. For instance, when a child begs his mother for candy and the mother refuses but instead proffers a better food for the child to eat while also encouraging him to grow more significant. The child gets excited and goes for the new alternative. In this way, the mother has been able to tap into his belief system without any form of duress. Hence, persuasion can also be used as a method of social control.

In politics and governing today, persuasion still retains its role as one of the essential means of influencing the populace's behavior, feelings, and commitment through the power of mass media. For instance, politicians sometimes use social media, television, radio, newspapers, and magazines to persuade people to sponsor their political campaigns. Persuasion in modern politics is also observed through the use of authority in such situations where opponents of one political party influence on cross carpet to the other party with different promises in the form of power and immunity. Also, the court still entertains the use of persuasion during the prosecution or defense of an accused.

Another way to see persuasion is through the intentional use of communication as a tool of conviction to change attitudes regarding an issue by transferring messages in a free choice atmosphere. The verbal, non-verbal, and visual forms of communication are manipulated just for the sole purpose of persuading an individual, group, or organization. Although communication is the most essential and versatile form in which persuasion is manifested, it is worthy to note that not all communication forms are intended to persuade. For instance, the celebration of a newly inaugurated president or governor circulated on the news cannot be classified as persuasion unless intended to impact the country's citizens or react in specific ways.

We go further to look at other possible definition of persuasion in the circular world.

Persuasion is a concept of influence that attempts to change a person's attitudes, intentions, motivations, beliefs, or behaviors. When a child begs his parent for candy and the parent says a big no to him, but the child insists on having candy even while knowing it might not be suitable for his health, persuasion is beginning to occur. The parent will try to proffer a better food for the child to eat instead of the candy. The child gets excited and goes for the new alternative. In this way, the parent has won a banter of persuasion.

On its own, persuasion is a branch of communication and popular as a method of social control. Hence, it is worthy of note that not all forms of communication intend to be persuasive. Persuasion is also a process by which a person's attitude and behaviors are influenced without harsh treatment by simple means of communication. Other factors can also determine a person's change in behavior or attitude, for example, verbal threats, a person's current psychological state, physical coercion, etc.

Having explained the meanings of persuasion, it can be observed that persuasion extends beyond a specific field as there is an intermingling of ideas from different study areas. However, communication and psychology seem clearly to be in use for persuasion to take place. While communication provides the model of how interlocutors in persuasion get messages understood, psychology provides the mental processes model during persuasion.

Now that we know both NLP and persuasion basics, we will now go more in-depth into detail about the subjects connecting to these two from this point and forward.

Chapter 1. Neuro-Linguistic Programming (NLP)

NLP is a fantastic art and science. It is an art since everyone gives what they are doing their own personal and stylish touch, which can never be conveyed with words or techniques. It is a science, and for outstanding results, there is a system and process to discover the models used for outstanding in-dividing in a region. This method is called patterning. In the field of education, guidance, and industry, the models, skills, and techniques discovered can increasingly be used to achieve more efficient communication, have substantial personal growth, and accelerate learning.

Have you ever done something so elegantly and successfully that your time will be cut short? Have there been moments when you were very pleased with what you were doing and how you handled it? The NLP shows you how to appreciate your achievements and arrange them to experience several more moments like this. It is a way of uncovering and unveiling your talent, a form of bringing out the best of yourself and others.

The NLP is a real ability that produces the outcomes we want in the world while at the same time valuing others in the process. It is the p of what distinguishes between the excellent and the nor-evil. It also leaves behind many extremely successful strategies on schooling, therapy systems, business, and therapies.

The History of NLP

The initial version of the NLP of today originated in the early 1970s. At the time, Richard Bandler was a student at the Santa Cruz University of California, met with John Grinder, assistant professor of linguistics.

Grinder, who was especially interested in advanced teaching techniques, was rapidly aware of Bandler's research and held a series of seminars in collaboration with him. Such seminars originally had the classification of group studies. But with growing Bandler and Grinder experience and expertise, the participants encountered more exciting transition processes ever. It culminated in an increasingly close relationship between Bandler and Grinder over the years.

They explored why well-known individual psychotherapists had so much success with their patients in their practice and on what basis this success was based. Several people treating the same patients with the same conditions have struggled to bring about these drastic improvements simultaneously. In Bandler and Grinder's original theory, they believed influential psychotherapists had a common or similar pattern of action in their work with people, based on which they might produce these excellent results. These standard or related behavior patterns are now known as NLP, or magic structure.

So, they started to investigate and evaluate the types of therapy used by the top therapists:

- Virginia Satir, an exceptional family therapist.

- Fritz Perl's, an innovative Gestalt therapist and founder of this direction of therapy, as well.

- Milton H. Erickson, a world-renowned hypnotherapist.

In doing so, the expectations of finding patterns and structures that could clarify these top therapists' success in coping with their clients were always driven.

Despite the three successful psychotherapists' diversity, after long and careful observation, Grinder and Bandler discovered that they used surprisingly similar basic patterns in their work with others. Grinder and Bandler put these basic patterns into writing, refined them, tried them out in their seminars with other students who agreed to do so. Finally, they developed an elegant model to achieve more effective communication, accelerated learning, personal change, and enjoyment, and joy in life. They called it NLP—Neuro-linguistic Programming:

"Neuro" because these are strategies that heavily involve the functions of our nervous system (brain + spinal cord + senses). The point is to perceive more precisely and more, to purposefully change unwanted feelings and behavior patterns in harmony with yourself.

"Linguistics" because it is also very much about the linguistic aspect. We maintain external communication with other people and internal communication with our fantastic "bio-computer"— our brain. Unfortunately, not all of the inputs that we make in this biocomputer are received. Therefore, advanced communication methods are also required here.

"Programming" means that we want to use systematic methods in all of this and not learn through trial and error. It's about discovering procedures and processes that can also be transferred to other areas and people. Many NLP techniques are content-free, which means that the same method can be used for headaches, a phobia, or to build an irresistible motivation. NLP describes procedures and processes that can and are effective regardless of the content.

Based on this approach, NLP developed in two complementary directions:

- In the first direction, as a process for discovering the pattern of brilliant achievements in every conceivable social area.

- The second direction is a compilation of effective ways of thinking and communication used by outstanding personalities in this field.

Beginnings of NLP

In the spring of 1972, Bandler himself offered a Gestalt therapy seminar, inspired by his studies' lack of real significance. It was possible for students in an advanced semester. He focused mainly on studying the therapeutic effects of gestalt work in a group and improving his theoretical skills in practice.

During these seminars, John Grinder became aware of Bandler's research, joining him and his exploration. From then on, both worked together on Bandler's workshops, with John Grinder, a beginner to counseling and psychotherapy.

Between 1972 and 1974, intense and productive cooperation took place, with Grinder benefiting from Bandler's knowledge of psychotherapy and Bandler's knowledge of linguistics.

This combination was particularly useful in modeling Virginia Satir's therapeutic masterpieces, Friedrich Perl's, and hypnotherapist Milton Erickson. When modeling, a person's unique skills are made learnable and accessible through systematic and accurate observation and questioning. Patterns and principles were developed so that interested people could also emulate the skills.

Bandler and Grinder were not primarily concerned with explaining something real but with discovering something useful for others. As proof of the success of their analyses and observations on Satir and Perl's, they saw evidence that in other people, they could achieve the same results as the person who modeled them.

In early 1974, both began designing the first meta-model structures with students held in Mission Street squat, Santa Cruz. To simply put, and the meta-model is a set of particular questions to uncover thinking processes and obtain in-depth knowledge. The starting point for research in the meta-model groups was that verbal communication between therapist and client is central to any therapeutic change work. Consequently, it was believed that common language patterns would crystallize and be cemented in Friedrich Perl's and Virginia Satir's verbal communication, making the dysfunctional processes conscious and causing change.

With John Grinder's linguistic context knowledge, both researchers succeeded in creating starting points for a model that allowed the targeted collection of information about a person's imaginary world. They modeled Perl's and Satir's critical linguistic skills and explained these constructs clearly and thus move them on.

From late 1974, Bandler and Grinder regularly participated in teaching seminars given by hypnotherapist Milton H. Erickson. Again, with the primary objective of researching Erickson's work with people, talking about his language patterns and actions. The findings were refined as with Satir and Perl's, reported in writing, tested for applicability in student groups, and integrated into the current knowledge base.

In 1974 and 1975, more formal communication models became the focus of group study. Since Perl's non-verbal actions often appeared to contribute significantly to the therapeutic impact achieved in addition to language behavior, the beneficial non-verbal elements were then specifically evaluated and attempted to address them. The resulting models were then used for both psychotherapy and daily contact.

Various types of procedures were used and revamped, leading, in addition to Perl's and Satir methods, to the current NLP shape. Bandler and Grinder published their first discoveries in four books from 1975 to 1977. These were:

In 1977, Grinder and Bandler held their first U.S. public seminars. The seminars were received very quickly. NLP's awareness has grown noticeably in the following years and is now used worldwide, especially in therapy, education, and management.

Bandler and Grinder developed reframing in 1982. It shows how one can contact unconscious parts, causing unwanted behaviors or disease symptoms. It enabled changes that were recently only conceivable under classical hypnosis.

1984 introduced the concept of submodalities, inventing one of NLP's most significant and impressive techniques. The submodalities represent a kind of brain programming language that everyone can use if they know the commands. People take information with their five senses, process it, and store it internally as events and thoughts represented in their senses, the so-called modalities. These modalities can, in turn, be specified more precisely, so it is possible to ask more precisely about an experience's inner picture. The fantastic thing about it is that it takes advantage of the fact that the human brain reacts to WHAT we think and how a person thinks, e.g., more in color pictures or black and white pictures.

James developed Time Line Therapy (Zeitlinie) in 1988. This method is particularly suitable for gently healing past traumatic experiences. Using the timeline, unconscious or repressed traumas causing physical or emotional problems can be found and mentally processed.

In 1990, Robert Dilts developed reimprinting to change our childhood's relational structures to limit beliefs and beliefs. An imprint is a decisive experience from which the person concerned has formed a belief or bundle of beliefs that are effective in his world. Such an imprint usually also includes an unconscious assumption of the role by other important people involved. The purpose of reimprinting is to find the missing resources, change the belief, and adapt the role model developed to the person's actual and acute circumstances.

Unlike popular belief, Grinder and Bandler did not create NLP alone. After thirty years of silence, a third colleague now goes public: Frank Pucelik.

Chapter 2. How NLP Works, Importance of NLP, and is NLP Effective?

How NLP Works?

If you are coming across this topic for the first time, NLP may appear or seem like magic or hypnosis. When a person is undergoing therapy, this topic digs deep into the patient's unconscious mind. It filters through different layers of beliefs and the person's approach or perception of life to deduce the early childhood experiences responsible for a behavioral pattern.

In NLP, it is believed that everyone has the resources that are needed for positive changes in their own lives. The technique adopted here is meant to help in facilitating these changes.

Usually, when NLP is taught, it is done in a pyramidal structure. However, the most advanced techniques are left for those multi-thousand-dollar seminars. An attempt to explain this complicated subject is to state that the NLP user (as those who use NLP will often call themselves) is always paying keen attention to the person they are working on/with.

Usually, many NLP users are therapists, and they are very likely to be well-meaning people. They achieve their aims by paying attention to those subtle cues like the eye's movement, flushing of the skin, dilation of the pupil, and subtle nervous tics. It is easy for an NLP user to determine the following quickly:

- The side of the brain that the person uses predominantly.

- The sense (smell, sight, etc.) that is more dominant in a person's brain.

- The way the person's brain stores and uses information.

- When the person is telling a lie or concocting information.

When the NLP user has successfully gathered all this information, they slowly and subtly mimic the client by taking on their body language and imitating their speech and mannerisms. They start to talk about language patterns that aim to target the client's primary senses. They will typically fake the social cues that will quickly make someone let their guard down to become very open and suggestible.

For example, when a person's sense of sight is their most dominant sense, the NLP user will use a very laden language with visual metaphors to speak with them. They will say things like: "do you see what I am talking about?" or "why not look at it this way?" For a person that has a more dominant sense of hearing, he will be approached with an auditory language like: "listen to me" or "I can hear where you're coming from."

The NLP user mirrors the body language and the other person's linguistic patterns to create a rapport. This rapport is a mental and physiological state that a human being gets into when they lose their social senses. When they begin to feel like the other person they are conversing with; it is just like them.

Once the NLP user has achieved this rapport, they will take charge of the interaction by leading it mildly and subtly. Thanks to the fact that they have already mirrored the other person, they will now begin to make some subtle changes to gain a particular influence on the person's behavior. It is also combined with some similar subtle language patterns, which lead to questions and a whole phase of some other techniques.

At this point, the NLP user will be able to tweak and twist the person to whichever direction they so desire. It only happens if the other person can't deduce that something is going on because they assume everything is happening organically or consent to everything.

In NLP, there is a belief in the need for nature's perfection of human creation, so every client is encouraged to recognize the senses' sensitivity and use them to respond to specific problems. NLP also believes that the mind can find cures for diseases and sicknesses.

Importance of NLP

NLP's effectiveness is focused on the idea that your mind and body are all the tools you need to improve your life and your world. It will help you to identify specific goals and act. And by analyzing your behaviors' changes, you can adjust them to produce better performance.

Some clinical studies suggest positive benefits to weight loss, reduced anxiety, and a healthy mood from Neuro-speaker programming. A specific investigation also reveals a positive impact on children's learning abilities with dyslexia, helping them improve their self-esteem by reducing their anxiety level. Here are the other importance or benefits of NLP:

As an adult, NLP lets you take responsibility for events that we feel we can't manage. A person can change his or her responses to past events and control their future through NLP. It is essential to be aware of people's body language in your inner circle and those you want to communicate with. NLP offers opportunities to use controlled and purposeful language. It helps you to monitor your life. With the same mind, you can't make the same mistakes and expect a different outcome. A Neuro-Linguistic (NLP) class is all about YOU; you are the subject. It is more important because it gives you more insight when dealing with individuals when dealing with yourself or yourself as an entity.

NLP helps you improve sales performance, income, health problems, better service to client, family, parenting, and all areas of your life. It allows you to become whole when your relationship with yourself and people is whole as an individual.

NLP helps you focus on your ideas, beliefs, and values. It allows you to understand your brain functions, how it develops patterns, how these behaviors become habits, how these habits become actions, and how these actions become outcomes.

The NLP application covers different professions and vocations in life. It is a highly competent tool for sales degrees, self-help and development experts, parents, teachers, communications, etc.

"You are all you ought to be, and all this is sufficient. Be proud of who you are and love who you are."

Is NLP Effective?

Based on valid, recognized, and established scientific research in sociology, linguistics, and psychology, NLP theories have been largely discredited as pseudo-science. The founders of NLP based their theories on sound scientific research. Still, the scientific community has repeatedly stated that the founders' comments and responses to inquiries have demonstrated that they do not understand the underlying theories they often cite in their work. Also, they have not produced any of their actual scientific evidence to support the claims made by NLP theorists or that their programming sessions bring about the changes they promise.

Mainstream psychology has established through clinical research, practice, and published works the reality of the subconscious mind and the importance of understanding its function to help alleviate, treat, or change harmful psychological developments in individuals. Cognitive-behavioral therapy (CBT) and traditional psychotherapy must meet with fairly rigorous professional standards and are based on proven methods and clinical psychology theories. At the same time, NLP's success record is less consistent and based more on anecdotal testimony.

NLP providers generally have a financial interest in promoting NLP's success, so their testimonials may or may not be accurate. Also, results among people who have completed NLP training sessions are mixed. Some studies have shown that patients who participate in NLP have improved psychological symptoms and a better quality of life. Still, most studies indicate little evidence that NLP can effectively treat any significant psychological disorders, such as anxiety, insomnia, or substance abuse.

However, while clinical studies have discredited NLP as a legitimate form of treatment for severe psychological illnesses, NLP continues to be part of the large, profitable industry that capitalizes on the demand for self-improvement literature. Tony Robbins, the contemporary self-help, self-improvement, and motivational speaking guru, trained with NLP's founders and continues to employ many of their ideas in his famous seminars.

Regardless of all the adverse press reports and scientific criticisms, NLP has spawned a global industry. Companies such as NLP Power, The NLP Center, The Empowerment Partnership, and the founders' own NLP University continue to advertise and promote their services on the internet and provide behavior modification training to a global audience. Many corporations and government agencies also send employees to NLP-based seminars to train leadership teams and sales staff. Thus, while the scientific foundations of NLP have been exposed and discredited, these organizations continue to attract followers and clients who see a benefit in the behavioral changes that result from associating with organizations that provide training in psychological and behavioral change.

Chapter 3. Components of NLP and NLP Techniques

Components of NLP

NLP's core philosophy is built on three essential components. From these components, other researchers and practitioners have expanded upon them. So long as these three components are respected, NLP is believed to work and be effective. To reach their maximum potential, practitioners need to pay close attention to how these pillars interact with one another.

Subjectivity

The first component, or core concept, is subjectivity. It is based on the fact that we all have different perceptions of the world around us. And while there are universal concepts that are believed and accepted, the fact of the matter is that we all have an experience that differs significantly.

Moreover, subjectivity is the basis of human experience. Therefore, we need to engage all of our senses to perceive the world as best we can. It is why educators who implement NLP seek to engage all five senses within the learning experience. That way, learners can get a good sense of the content they are trying to internalize.

Consciousness

NLP is predicated because the human psyche is built on a dual-layer of consciousness and unconsciousness. In this manner, the human psyche uses consciousness to express rationality for the things that we do daily. On the flip side, unconsciousness is the automatic manifestation of the built-in programming that we have accrued throughout your evolution.

Learning

Learning occurs when the conscious internalization of the world around us is achieved through the senses' perception. When a person can internalize content or their particular perception of the experiences they live, they can transform this into learning. It is why experience is crucial to the effectiveness of NLP. Unless a human is unable to experience the world, meaningful learning cannot fully take place.

NLP Techniques and How They Work

Neuro-Linguistic Programming (NLP) tells you that emotions and experiences guide people on their planet's view. It tells us that what you currently see isn't the critical world but a distorted representation supported your beliefs, perceptions, values, and other variables. NLP techniques will help you integrate aspects of your life, improve your quality, and understand how people work. Discover how to use these NLP techniques to enhance communication skills and emotional intelligence that you can use to regulate your life and mind.

Anchoring

The anchoring technique in NLP is important to tug up a particular emotion or put yourself into a specific psychological state, which may be used on yourself or somebody else. It works by integrating emotion with a physical movement, and the anchor laying dubs it. For example, if you decided to tug the thrilling feeling, you'd start by brooding about the days you have been euphoric. You'd wish to tell the account of what went on in your head that led to the present moment. Mention how it feels and enter an excellent deal of detail. Remember the instant, the emotions.

First, confine your right to your left index and middle fingers. Squeeze them twice. Mention your special moment on the second squeeze and strive to feature the feeling. Describe once more how you are feeling, how you think, and clap your hands twice. Let the nice and cozy feeling double once you clap the second time. Roll in the hay continuously for five times. You'll use those gestures to regain your feeling of happiness. You'd use a fast touch of the arm to secure them if you were to try this to a different man.

Meta Model

The methodology of the meta-model of NLP is usually wont to understand other individuals' concerns. It could even be wont to support others to possess a better understanding of their issues. The aim is to dismantle the conversation, assist you in achieving the basis explanation for the difficulty, and fix it. The response is consciously or unconsciously understood when someone features a question, but the only solution is some things that they are doing not like. The shortage of uncertainty allows the crisis to persist, anticipating that there'll finally be a replacement solution. You'll help them develop how by deconstructing the way someone explains their question.

Mirroring

One of the foremost relevant NLP strategies you ought to learn is mirroring. It'll be very beneficial to be good at mirroring. It's been quite hard to hate someone who knows the way to do that act. Moreover, it's the replication of the individual you interact with (i.e., his/her behaviors). While being subtle and typically subconscious, this simulation is complete. Copying somebody's speech patterns, visual communication, vocabulary style, speed, rhythm, pitch, voice, and volume are ways you'll do that.

Framing

The technique of NLP framing is employed to affect the rise or decrease of the emotional feeling significantly. It is an excellent way to use alongside most of the others. You are going to experience good and bad moments in life. These should enable you to be ready to learn and grow in your life. Nonetheless, memories haven't any feelings connected to them. Such separation occurs because memories and thoughts exist in several parts of the brain. Therefore, at present, you'll experience feelings, then you'll be ready to remember them. The hippocampus is that the brain part that's liable for LTM storage. The amygdala is the brain's portion that regulates feelings. The amygdala will offer you a fast-little reminder of what you feel once you recall a memory from the hippocampus. Simply because of that, the feeling that's important to a selected memory is often modified.

Pattern Interruption

Interruption of the pattern is usually wont to preserve words during a listener's subconscious. One great technique to pair with others is that this technique. To try this, you've got to draw the listener's thoughts into a series or pattern form. When the model gets out of control before finishing the shape, you would like to require them out of the template for a critical juncture. The listener's unconscious is meant to embody the pattern while the conscious mind is overwhelmed at that moment. You'll change the way you think that check out the past, and consider your life with a replacement way of thinking by learning NLP. It can help to enhance your communication skills and enhance your emotional intelligence.

Chapter 4. The Swish Pattern

The Swish Pattern is your answer to powerful and constant change. It is one of the most widely known and widely used NLP tools, and it helps people genuinely create their ideal self and eliminate negative behaviors. Using visualization, the Swish Pattern allows you to take the old images and behaviors you have developed over the years and replace them with powerful, dynamic. All-around better images and behaviors that work for the new ideal life you want to build.

First, though, you need to understand what visualization is:

Visualization

Visualization has gotten a bad rep, mostly because it has been tied up with Oprah's new age movement and the Law of Attraction. Everything can be yours if you just sit down and visualize that it is yours. And that is left behind many bitter and angry people who are ready to say visualization is not good. But, visualization is a tool used by athletes, politicians, and billionaire business people who want to get more and more from their life. Which is all to say many people are wrong.

One of the essential foundational tools for change when it comes to using NLP is visualization. To powerfully use all the NLP tools, you will need to understand what visualization is and how to use it, especially when using the Swish Pattern.

Power of Visualization

Dr. Biasiatto did a study at the University of Chicago, where he took three groups of people and tested their free-throw ability. He took note of each of their scores, and then he had one group practice their free throws for an hour every day for a month. The second group makes them visualize, making free throws for a little bit every day. In the third group, he had to do nothing at all.

In the end, the group that did nothing improved in no way whatsoever. The first group that practiced an hour a day improved their free throws by 24%. The visualization group was just 1% short of people who practiced for an hour a day. They improved at nearly the same rate as those practicing every day through merely the power of mental rehearsal.

Study after study has confirmed that the brain processes a visualized event the same way a real event happens. Athletes who visualize their playing see their muscle fibers activate and their brain process as if they are doing it. Some of the world's wealthiest and most influential people talk about using visualization to enhance their success, get better ideas, and achieve faster.

Visualizing is real. It works when you know how to do it. But, there are a few things that usually trip people up that do not have to trip you up. First and foremost, you do not have to be able to see anything. It is so important because many people think if they are not visual thinkers, then the visualization will not work for them, so they never try it.

Also, though, this will come if you practice visualization enough, your brain will learn to start creating images, and you'll feel a lot better about the whole process. But for many people, they are not visual thinkers, so they're initially just not seeing anything.

It's okay. You do not have to see anything to visualize (as weird as that sounds). Your brain will create experiences for you; if you focus on it, you will access other areas of your body, whether kinesthetic, verbal or anything else.

You will develop the feelings and the skills you are looking for. Now that you understand visualization, let us talk about the Swish Pattern.

The Swish Pattern

The Swish Pattern is a life changer that helps people with weight loss, smoking cessation, better habits, a healthy self-image, a more meaningful and better life. The thing is that you already have your ideal-self likely built inside of you. You know what your life would look like if you did not have your problems and what amazing things could happen with your life once those problems were solved.

You probably have a self-image of yourself that is far and away from your ideal, one that has been built by those problems weighing you down and working on you. It is these two images that you can leverage to make significant changes in your life.

Swish Pattern Step by Step

Step 1: Recognize Your Automatic Reactions

Images, thoughts, emotions, and a host of other things can cause you to have an adverse reaction. Whether you are reaching for a cigarette or a muffin, or it is making you yell and scream, or retreat and cower. We all respond to certain stimuli in remarkably consistent ways with our character that probably does not always help us be the best version of ourselves that we would want to be. You want to find that automatic response for whatever behavior or emotion or anything else that you want to fix. Once you do, you want to narrow down all the images, emotions, and anything else that forms in your mind when you respond in those automatic fashions.

You want to create an ideal image, a simple, powerful one that connects with your emotional state. It should be inspiring, exciting, and something that should make you want to change. You want to create this image focusing on your life would be like without whatever negative automatic response you have.

Once you have these two things, you want to create an image of yourself disassociated from both of these things, almost as if you're watching these two images from a distance, looking at them, admiring them.

Step 2: Determine the Cause of the Negative Image

As we said, you have automatic responses, and hopefully, you will have found them. Now, it is time to isolate what causes these automatic responses. Something brings these negative states to the forefront of your mind. Negative behaviors do not come from anywhere. Find that trigger. Ask yourself, "What Occurs Before This Negative State Begins?" This way, you can imagine the automatic response happening from the trigger and be prepared to create an alternative response to this event in the future.

Step 3: Prepare for Displacement

Take the positive image that you made initially, make it the size of a postage stamp in your mind, and place it on the corner of your developed negative image. You will want to notice a few things from its placement in the corner of the image. Its brightness, it is strength, and everything else that makes it stand out.

Step 4: Swish the Two Images

Now you are going to swish the images back and forth. Making a Swish sound can help because it gives your brain something else to engage with. Imagine the images switching places—the positive one growing more prominent, brighter, and more colorful. The negative one shoots off into the distance of your mind, disappearing and becoming nothing but a memory.

Notice how the further an image travels in your mind, the further the malicious behavior feels a part of you. More importantly, notice how, when the positive image gets brighter, your positive image can feel better.

Step 5: Repeat the Process

Keep repeating the swishing. Bring the old image back to the front of your mind; notice it as it loses color, as it gets blurry, as it begins to lose more and more of its power. You will notice the more powerful image continuing to glow brighter and brighter in the corner, almost as if it cannot be contained.

Keep the process going until the negative image has become tattered, black and white, blurry, and no longer packs the same emotions with it that it once did.

Step 6: Test It

Think about your negative emotion, think about the trigger, and find out if it is now replaced with that more powerful image that you want.

The Swish Pattern is a powerful tool, and it can completely liberate you from your negative behaviors and negative beliefs if you let it and you work it. It is there to help you genuinely transform how you live. You should notice improvement within a few days of using it, especially if you do it every day for a few days until it becomes part of your unconscious. There is no such thing as a transformation without actual work. You are going to have to work at it. The people who complain about the Swish Pattern do so because they thought they could do it once and forget it. But, that is not how it works. That is not how life works. But if you do it few a few days in a row, keep testing it; find where you're feeling weak with it. Within a week, you should see a clear improvement in your malicious behavior and see a positive transformation.

It works, and it works well. As you move through life, consistently trying to make yourself the best version of yourself possible, you will need to use this technique every time you want to end a malicious behavior. The more negative behaviors, beliefs, and emotions you can eliminate from your life, the better your overall life will be. The more you use this, the faster it will work, and the more powerful this technique will become in helping you create the behaviors and strengths you want in your life. You can install everything you want inside of you. You can make your life as exciting and memorable as possible.

The best thing about the swish pattern is that you can do it just about anywhere, and you can control the process. No need for audiotapes or some outside person guiding you through the process; no, you can be in complete control and have full power over yourself.

Start the process now and figure out what you want to change and what negative behaviors you want to eliminate from your life for good. Then create a list of desired behaviors and start to craft out everything that you want to do with your life and what your life will be like if you had these fantastic new behaviors instead of the negative ones you want to get rid of.

The more you design out your amazing future and your amazing life, the more you craft out the opportunity to create something marvelous for yourself to take over.

Chapter 5. Hypnosis

Hypnosis is a position of consciousness that involves focused attention, together with reduced peripheral awareness characterized by the participant's increased ability to respond to suggestions given. Every person has a waking state, a state when they know that they are awake, alert, alive, and in the universe.

What happens is that your attention becomes more and more focused, and your awareness of your environment diminishes. Your attention has more focused on what is inside and lesser on what is occurring outside. It makes you much more aware of your internal images, feelings, and thoughts and less aware of things going on in your surroundings. Usually, it's so pleasant for many people, enjoyable and very relaxing.

Highly imaginative people are usually easier to hypnotize: they have an intense experience of both nature and art. Psychopaths tend to be immune to hypnosis because psychopaths tend to have restricted emotions, but many people are easily hypnotized. Being in a hypnotic state is a regular aspect of human life. Often, creative people use guided imagination in their daily routine without necessarily realizing it as a hypnotic technique.

Three Stages of Hypnosis

Hypnosis is more of an ability than a disadvantage unless you are often hypnotically governed by an external force. Three stages are recognized in the hypnosis field:

Induction

It is the first stage involved in hypnosis. Before a subject undergoes full hypnosis, the subject is introduced to the hypnotic induction technique. For many years, hypnotic induction was used to put the participant into their hypnotic trance, but the definition has altered some modern times. Some of the non-state theorists have comprehended this stage a bit differently. Instead, the theorists understand this stage as the technique to enhance the subjects' expectations of what will happen—defining the role that they will play, getting their attention to concentrate on the right direction and any of the steps that are required to lead the subject into the appropriate direction of hypnosis.

Various induction methods can be applied during hypnosis. The most used method is the Braidism technique. The Braids technique has a few variations, like the Stanford Hypnotic Susceptibility Scale, which is the most applied research tool in the hypnosis field.

For you to apply the Braidism technique, you will have to follow the following steps:

- First, take any object that you can find bright, for example, a watch case, hold it between your middle, fore, and thumb fingers on the left hand. Hold the object somewhere above the forehead to produce a lot of strain on the eyelids and eyes. During the process so that the subject can maintain a fixed stare on the object at all times.

- Secondly, the hypnotist should then explain to the subject that they should keep their eyes often fixed on the object. The subject will also be required to focus theirs mindfully on the idea of that specific object. The subject should not be allowed to think of any other thing or let their mind wander, or else, the process will not be successful.

After some time, the subject's eyes will start to dilate. With some more time, the subject will begin to assume a wavy motion. If the subject involuntarily closes their eyelids when the fore and middle fingers of the right hand are carried from their eyes to the object, they are in a trance. If this is not the case, the subject will be required to start the process again: you should ensure that you let the subject know that they are to let their eyes close once the fingers are carried in a similar motion back towards the eyes again. It will get the subject to go into an altered state of the mind or hypnosis.

Suggestion

At first, the term suggestion was not used. Instead, Braid defined this stage as the act of having the conscious mind of the subject concentrate on one dominant and central idea. Braid did this to reduce or trigger the various regions' physiological functioning on the subject's body. Braid then started to emphasize applying various non-verbal and verbal forms of suggestion to get the subject into the mind's hypnotic condition. These would involve using waking suggestions as well as self-hypnosis. Hippolyte Bernheim, another hypnotist, emphasized the hypnosis process's physical condition over the psychological process that included verbal suggestions. According to Hippolyte, hypnosis is the induction of a physical state that is peculiar and which will enhance the susceptibility of the suggestion to the subject. He always stated that the hypnotic condition that is induced would assist in facilitating the suggestion.

Modern hypnotism applies various suggestions to be successful, such as direct verbal suggestions, insinuations, metaphors, non-verbal suggestions, and other figures of speech that are non-verbal. Some of the non-verbal suggestions that may be used would include mental imagery, voice tonality, and physical manipulation.

One of the distinctions made in the types of suggestions offered to the subject includes those suggestions delivered with permission and more authoritarian. One of the aspects that have to be considered regarding hypnosis is the difference between conscious and unconscious minds. Several hypnotists view this stage to communicate directed to most of the participant's conscious minds.

Susceptibility

It has been observed that people will react differently to hypnosis. Some will find that they can easily fall into a hypnotic trance and don't have to put much effort into the process. Others will find that they can get into the hypnotic trance, but only after a prolonged period and with some effort applied. Still, other people will find that they cannot get into the trance and, even after constant efforts, will not reach their goals.

One thing that has been found about the various subject's susceptibility is that this part remains unchanging. If you have gotten into a trance easily, you will likely be the same way for the rest of your life. On the contrary, if you have challenges teaching your hypnotic star of mind and have never been experiencing hypnotized, then it is probably that you never will.

Two types of victims are considered to be highly susceptible to the effects of hypnotism. These include:

- Fantasizers

- Associates

Fantasizers will have a high score on the absorption scales; they will block out easily the real world's stimuli without the use of hypnosis. They spend a lot of time daydreaming, they grew up in an environment where imaginary play was encouraged, and they had imaginary pals when they were in their childhood.

Associates will always come from childhood abuse or trauma; they found ways to forget their trauma and escape into numbness. When they daydream, it is more in terms of going blank instead of creating fantasies. Both dissociation and fantasizers score highly on the tests of hypnotic susceptibility.

Two groups of people with the highest hypnotism rates include those suffering from dissociative identity disorder and post-traumatic stress disorder.

Effects of Hypnosis

In a trance state, your ability to think logically and critically reduces. You tend to accept any information that is given to you without thinking if it's reasonable and rational or not.

People in a hypnotic state are suggestible. They tend to consent uncritically to any suggestions given to them. Even the strong-willed people can be hypnotized and made to do things that they wouldn't normally do.

Conscious decision making, independent judgment, and rational analysis are all suspended. It is a bonus for leaders who, after all, don't want their members thinking of themselves. Hypnosis is an incredibly powerful set of tools to influence others and manipulate others to do things that violate their ethics and morals.

What Manipulators Say

It is exciting that most leaders usually claim that people can't be made to do things against their will, even when applying mind control hypnosis.

The members are programmed to agree to whatever the leaders say. Therefore, the members will tend to accept the idea. Implicit in the idea is that if the person does something, they do it of their own volition.

When you make your own decisions, you believe more firmly and more committed to the outcome, and the actions and effects of your decision last longer.

Myths About Hypnosis

You should remember that hypnosis is not often a closed-eye process. It's not compulsory to have your eyes closed to be in a trance. Have you ever tried to be on a trip or journey, and when you reach your destination, you do not even remember much of the journey? That is an example of a trance that you were in.

People in a trance state who are driving while their eyes are entirely open and performing; if they see a person in front braking, there's no difficulty in braking themselves and doing what is necessary to avoid accidents. Many have the idea that there are unique hypnotic words to trigger trance. Hypnosis can be triggered in normal-sounding conversations, using the daily words.

Chapter 6. Brainwashing

If you talk to someone and ask them what they think brainwashing is, they may reply that they know because this is a topic that many people have heard about. But most people don't have a full understanding of how this kind of mind control can work. And if you are trying to fight off someone using dark psychology, you must make sure that you understand this topic.

Brainwashing will be the slow process of taking the ideas that a victim has about their identity and their beliefs and then replacing them with new ideas to suit the manipulator's purpose. Brainwashing can occur in a narrow and broad context. For example, a brainwasher could use the techniques to control one person or use those techniques to control a more extensive group's minds all at once.

The Process of Brainwashing

The starting point of brainwashing is the social circumstances and the mental state of the victim. It will be the basis for the rest of the process, and if the manipulator cannot figure this part out, then the brainwashing session won't be successful. Brainwashing is not a process that is going to work out for everyone. It will require an adequate identification of a person looking for something or someone who has a void they are trying to fill.

It brings us to an important point. Who is the ideal victim for a brainwasher? People who have had their existing reality shaken up because of some recent events are excellent brainwashers' targets. If you have lost someone you are close to or had another dramatic or traumatic event in your life, then you may be more susceptible to brainwashing.

Once the brainwasher has found their victim, the process of brainwashing can begin. Contrary to the popular image you may have in your mind about a brainwasher, this person will often come across as someone rational, friendly, and calm. Someone who seems to have their lives together in a way the victim wishes they could have their own. Visualize how it would feel if you were homeless and a celebrity you admired befriended you. It is often how the process of meeting the brainwasher is going to feel for the victim.

The brainwasher is going to get to work right away. The first step for them is to create a rapport and trust between them and the victim. It is going to be done with superficial and deep similarities. The superficial similarities could involve some surface-level preferences, something like enjoying the same food or sport as the other person.

They will then move on to a deeper level of rapport, some that could involve a more in-depth shared experience that they had in the past. The brainwasher will most likely fake these, convincingly, to create these bonds. If the victim shares with the brainwasher that they lost a close relative in the past, then the brainwasher is suddenly going to have a similar story to share with the victim.

This false connection and warmth emotionally are not the only thing that is going to occur. The brainwasher wants to cement that new bond as quickly as possible. It is not unconventional for them to provide favors and gifts to their victim. They could send them a gadget or some other item they may find useful. They may treat the victim to a meal. It is to create a sense of gratitude and indebtedness from the victim to that brainwasher. It is going to soften up a lot of the resistance that the victim may experience.

After the resistance has been stripped away a little bit, the other step will be a sort of romantic presentation. It will involve the brainwasher slowly and increasingly offer a solution to any problems that the victim recently opened up about. It is not going to be a big hard push or sell. Instead, the brainwasher knows how to do this in an offhand and casual way to make sure they don't deal with any negative experiences by pressing the victim. This solution will always be the personality, ideology, or cult that the brainwasher is working to make the victim convert.

When these steps are done correctly, the initial stages will leave the victim wanting more. The victim will want more information and more understanding of the solution that the brainwasher hints at. The brainwasher may even withhold some of this information initially, treating it as something that the victim needs to do some work to attain. Doing this is to push the victim to seek out and accept the information they are eventually going to hear.

After the victim has had some time being spoon-fed snippets of this belief system, and they have shown they will respond well to them, the brainwasher will be careful to reveal the right information at the right time. It is a concept that is called a gradual revelation or milk before meat. It will include the presentation of an easy to accept idea before the controversial idea is revealed.

For example, if the brainwasher is trying to convert the victim over to religious terrorism, they would not start with the terrorism part. They may initially start focusing on the fact that God loves the victim, something that the victim is likely to accept. The more objectionable ideas, such as God wants you to blow yourself up, are ones that are saved until much after in the process. Once the victim has accepted that last part, then this brainwashing session is at a point of no return.

In this situation, you may be curious why the victim is still engaging with the brainwasher, especially when these more objectionable ideas become apparent. There are three main reasons:

The brainwasher has worked on the vulnerable victim. They feel a strong sense of liking the brainwasher, and they want to get the brainwasher's approval.

The victim has invested some time, and in some cases, money, in the process up to this point. It is often known as the sunk cost fallacy. The victim will feel like it is terrible to throw away all the hard work and money they have put into the process.

During this process, the brainwasher has been amassing many sensitive and secretive information on the victim. The brainwasher is often willing to hold this information over the victim to keep the victim on the right path.

The Impact of Brainwashing

The above analysis that we did about brainwashing is going to show how severe this technique can be. It is changing the victim's beliefs and inner identity, and this can be a big deal. Sure, the manipulator will get what they want out of the process, but the victim will lose out on their real identity and often gets so far into the process that they aren't sure what went wrong.

Many different impacts will come with brainwashing after the process is completed. The first one is a loss of identity. Many ideologies and cults feature that the people who go through the initiation process are given a new name. It helps the psyche of the person to detach from their old identity altogether. They can believe things and even do things they would never have done in the past because that older adult they were no longer exists. When this process is carried out the proper way, it can leave a victim feeling like all the parts of their old identity are no longer real or permanent and that they have woken up from a nightmare.

Post-traumatic stress disorder, or PTSD, can sometimes be a hallmark of those who managed to escape or rescued from a situation where they were brainwashed. The victims of these brainwashing endeavors will show some of the same psychological and physical signs as war veterans who were right in the battle. The severity of this traumatic aftermath shows that this type of process, of the manipulator getting more control over the victim, could harm the victim as much as if they went to war.

Brainwashing is something that can have a lasting impact. There are plenty of examples of rescued individuals or who managed to escape from their brainwashing situation, who then went back to that situation of their own free will. Even when they were able to leave the brainwashing and controlling environment they were in, the legacy that came with that process was done so well and ran so deep in their mind that the victim wants to return to it. It shows the power of using this brainwashing process and how much a manipulator could gain.

Chapter 7. How to Use NLP for in Sales

We are all on sale, believe it or not. When was the last time you had to sell an idea you had to your boss or your colleagues or make a proposal to increase your project budget? When was the last time you had to convince your kids to do something they were supposed to do? Whether you sell a product, service, concept, or influence others to achieve the desired result, you sell.

The following 5-step sales process seems to be a simple framework to use and remember:

- Establish and maintain a rapport.

- Understand your client or potential client.

- Define the need/define the value.

- Need/value link to your product or service.

- Close the sale.

Neuro-linguistic Programming is the study of excellence and excellent communication and how to reproduce it. Your ability to communicate effectively is the key to your success in any business interaction. So, let's look at each step of the 5-step sales process and see how NLP fits in.

Establish and Maintain a Rapport

Keeping eye contact while talking or listening to another person is one way to stay connected. Leaning or bending forward and tilting a bit your head to the side while listening shows that you are entirely listening and engaged to the person you're talking to. Uniting and reflecting body, voice, and words is another way to create and maintain relationships. Any resistance you encounter means that you have not established enough relationships and an excellent indicator to go back and build an additional connection. Making a rapport is the first step to getting better results in sales or any communication interaction.

Understand Your Client or Potential Client

The best way to understand your client or prospect is to ask many open questions. Asking questions will allow you to know your client/potential client better and will allow you to identify if it is necessary for your product or service. Find out what is important to them, how they think and process information. Observe their eye patterns as they answer questions to see where they are going to access private information. Look at the main words you use most often. Do they prefer visual words and descriptors such as "I see, can I imagine," or do they incline to the auditory words "I hear what you think," "it sounds true." Or are they more appropriate with kinesthetic phrases like "I understand what you are saying"? I feel your passion. "If you understand the needs of the client or potential client and understand their communication style and preferences, you will be better prepared to communicate with them in a way that works best for them.

Define the Need/Define the Value

Once you have determined the need, you need to define a value. Do you realize it would be useful to solve your problem or improve the situation? Reinforce your value proposition by asking something like, "So it would be useful to answer that, right? Is it something that would interest you or not?" It is an important problem because they may have a need but see no value in solving it. Most sellers spend 80% of their time on people who don't buy. You want potential clients/buyers to buy while ensuring that the value solves their problem is crucial to your sales pitch.

Connect Need/Value to Your Product or Service

You don't sell a product or service in the sales process. You sell emotion. We believe it is our sound mind that makes the decision, but the fact is that all of our memories, feelings, and emotions are stored in our unconscious. Furthermore, the more significant part of our choices is made subliminally. Connecting with your client or client's sentiment is the key to your ability to close a sale successfully. For example, potential buyers looking to buy a new home can see the value of a locker room. You associate it with the sensation she will feel when she wakes up in the morning, approaches her, and feels good when she sees and chooses clothes quickly in the morning. This feeling will connect her to the house they are selling.

Close

If you have successfully followed steps 1 through 4, closing should be smooth. Just ask for a purchase or order. Take advantage of the sale to the end and look for a win-win opportunity.

Chapter 8. How to Use NLP in Relationships

In this part, we will know how NLP can be beneficial to healthy relationships. We will learn what excellent and fulfilling relationships are based on and built upon. We will explore techniques that can strengthen relationships and those that can help us establish healthy relationships. We will talk about the benefits or importance of our mental health and readiness before entering any partnership or relationship and possible outcomes associated with having and not having these factors.

Once you have decided what you want, now is the time to enter into a relationship and have covered your predetermining factors. Now you can begin to open up to the possibilities of finding the right person. Here is when rapport becomes essential. What is rapport? It's your similarities and likeness with someone you are interested in entering a relationship with. It's also the establishment of trust with that person. With rapport, many individual factors can be used for determining compatibility. Some of these are personality types, values, beliefs, culture, political ideologies, interests, religious beliefs, etc. Of course, physical characteristics, such as gender and body types, need to be considered. However, some features can't be overaccentuated because it will mimic the other and cause a loss of rapport.

The rapport established initially, the reasons for your attraction to your partner, and his or her attraction to you must be kept at the forefront of each partner's mind throughout the relationship. It all too familiar for people to enter relationships with guns blazing, meaning being the perfect partner, only to begin to relax and change once the relationship has been established. One partner, or both, will use all available techniques to get the other to enter into a relationship. Once they are in that relationship, the other partner believes they can initially tone down what they were doing. It is one of the typical reasons for relationships ending. Keep in mind, the reasons for someone falling for you are the same reasons that will make them want to stay with you. If you remove the reasons for their attraction, they have no reasons to stay with you. Often, we see children born of relationships used as new reasons, but this does not work. It leads the partnership to morph into, what be, a business relationship. There will be no real emotional connection in the relationship and, even though that couple may remain together, they will lack the comforts and fulfillment of needs they desire.

Now you have identified what you want, making sure the timing is right, and have met that special someone. Now, what do you do? You need to ensure that your significant other feels the same about you. There are several ways in which a person can see that they are loved by the other. These ways should be identified at the relationships beginning. A few methods are by what the other person buys and places he or she takes you. There are also things such as how they touch you, the looks they give, or what they say. Identification of these is essential as they can gauge the continuance of love throughout the relationship.

The best way to determine how you can best assure your partner that you love them is by doing what they tend to do for you. For instance, if your partner puts her arm around you at times to assure you of her love and affection, you can bet that if you do the same, she will believe that you do love and appreciate her. We don't tend to do things to or for others, especially those whom we care about the most, that we wouldn't want to be done to us. Although this is commons sense, it's also an excellent method to gauge or determine how your significant other feels about you. As the relationship progresses, this will come naturally and will take much less conscious effort. Be sure not to allow these things to stop just because the relationship is no longer new.

NLP has devised a few strategies to determine areas in relationships. Areas such as attraction, love, and desire are all strategized with NLP techniques. First, you must know your partner. It means that you should know what those subtle gestures and tones of voice your partner will display depending on how they feel. Know what your partner fears and what he or she wants. You will pick up ideas as to how to carry these things out by merely learning your partner. Be sure never to use this knowledge for manipulation. There isn't a positive outcome in relationships where manipulation takes place.

One technique you can use to ensure that your partner is in love with you and wants you is to remove yourself from his or her presence temporarily. It does not mean that you can tell your wife that you are going to the store for a lottery ticket to not return for a week. However, in short time frames, absence can signal want or lack thereof. Just like the cliché, absence makes the heart grow fonder; this is built on the same premise. When using these kinds of tactics, please never overuse them. Here is some advice. If you are an insecure person needing constant approval and reassurance that you are loved, you should take care of that issue before entering a serious relationship. If not, you will not be the right partner. If your shortcoming does not end the relationship, it could lead it to become a codependent partnership or, at the very least, a very unhealthy relationship. Again, you must first make sure that you are the right candidate for entering into a relationship before taking that other step.

With relationships, you are not merely selling yourself to another, and then the job is over. It's a continuing process forever. Never relax and believe that you have your partner and aren't going anywhere, no matter what you may or may not do. You should always be selling yourself, your worth, compassion, and desire for your partner.

Think of this; You meet someone at the beach or any spot you can imagine. You are both at that exact place at that same time. You may both have everything in common too. However, both you and the other person took different routes to that spot and lived through different circumstances while on the way. Even though you both find yourselves to be at the same point and with the same characteristics, you took different paths there. It means that it's likely that you are not both going to react or respond to every event the same, and those events may lead you to go in different directions. Another way to look at this; you may both like the same sports team. The difference is why each of you has this opinion of that team. One of you may be a graduate from that university, while the other just picked last season's champions. It probably means that the school's alumnus is less likely to decide that they no longer favor that team. Regardless of the possible ways, the ending remains the same. What does this mean? Are we all just merely at life's mercy and subject to emotional trauma at the drop of a hat? Not exactly. Although we may not be able to change the situation when finding ourselves here, we can know why. First, don't give up. Do whatever you can to carry both you and your partner through the tough spot in your relationship, and you may find that you both were able to beat the odds and remain together.

Let's look at what it means to have taken different routes. The recently mentioned scenarios were only metaphors. The location isn't an actual place but a specific state of mind and life situation. Regardless of the spectrum of commonalities you and your partner may or may not have, you both will respond and react to things differently. One of you may be able to brush something, such as a traumatic event, off, but the other cannot do that. Let's look at this. Both you and your wife have religious faith. It is one of the main commonalities you found of yourselves that led to your relationship. Then down the road, your wife either endures a traumatic event or meets an influential person, either causing a dramatic shift in her religious ideologies. What was once the main glue that kept you together has deteriorated to where there is no more left. Not only does she no longer agree with your religious faith, but her newfound beliefs also contradict what you believe. What do you do when faced with this situation? Both of you are firmly holding to your individual beliefs and not willing to waiver. Both accuse the other of being naïve. Neither of you is terrible people, but you are no longer finding the same rapport you once had.

You both joined the relationship only after taking the proper steps and exercised due caution in choosing the other as a mate. Even though this was done, life didn't care about that. Circumstances led to the separation of you and your partner's beliefs, and both of you are much too committed to your independent ideas to compromise them. Therefore, you are now at constant odds, and the negativity within the relationship grows stronger each day. One day, it will lead to resentment and even hate. You have taken the necessary steps in attempting to salvage the relationship to no avail. So, as the very last resort, you decide to part ways. It happens every day.

Like the baggage we carry due to prior bad relationships, we have lessons learned and unique ways of dealing with specific issues based on these lessons. The best thing to do is know what and how things are going, and this can give you a good idea as to what is about to come.

To conclude this guide, NLP is essential and beneficial in the relationship. It isn't just with the beginning of the union but throughout its entirety. You must first know yourself, and then using NLP; you can learn your partner. Knowing your partner can prove invaluable in maintaining a healthy and long relationship. Also, the relationship will be much more fulfilling to both parties. Remember that severe and personal relationships prove beneficial in many areas in life and isn't limited to just the partnership. It's beneficial for both of you as a couple, as individuals, and as part of society.

Chapter 9. NLP in Business

NLP enhances negotiation skills and selling skills. Clients who use NLP in the business report that their managers are excellent coaches, motivators, and influencers.

NLP multiplies excellence in any field. It is a skill known as modeling in NLP; it incorporates all other intermediate skills. It is beneficial in a business organization if, for example, business took good employees from each field and brought them together. The work done will be excellent.

NLP helps to improve communication while doing business. During communication, there is the use of verbal and non-verbal cues. Using NLP, one will be able to understand the spoken and unspoken language of clients and prospects.

It helps one to emulate the successful efforts of other businesses easily. NLP teaches one to understand how successful people work and converse. One can then emulate those using NLP strategies to copy those successes to fit their businesses.

NLP gives one sales staff mind-reading abilities. It enables them to understand non-verbal cues and eye movements, allowing them to answer clients' questions and provide useful information about the products. They also understand how a client feels about the product in question, making it easier for them to close sales.

NLP improves negotiation skills. Negotiation is a critical requirement in the business world—negotiation with vendors, employees' marketers, advertising firms, and many more. With

NLP negotiation skills, everyone in the business will be more effective and persuasive.

NLP boosts morale. Why wouldn't one's morale be boosted if everyone in the company or office knows how well and effectively you communicate? One can make themselves apparent as well as able to relate with everyone in the office. It makes the workplace much more fun since there is a better understanding of one another.

NLP is the best client service tool. NLP helps to understand clients' complaints and suggestions after a sale. One can discern if a client is complaining because of awful client service or if he or she is having a bad day. When one's client care can understand the client's non-verbal cues, he will be able to deal with the angry client and make them happy to come again.

NLP can be so useful in boosting your entrepreneurial pursuits. It helps build skills in teamwork, coaching, sales, productivity, personal development, and leadership. For NLP to be useful, there must be potential for growth, and human interaction should be present.

NLP is a useful tool when you are setting and working toward achieving your goals. When you are in a business state, you must set your goals, which are supposed to be achievable, intelligent, meaningful, and measurable. For instance, it will not be realistic for you to set a goal to earn millions of dollars within a month without having logical ways to achieve your goal. Thus, using NLP, it is possible to set and achieve goals for your business. Using NLP will help you change your way of thinking and speaking and motivate you to take appropriate actions toward achieving your goal.

When you are in a business, sometimes you become stressed, but if you apply NLP techniques, it is possible to have a happier and more fulfilling life. NLP includes studying successful people's steps to achieve success, and these successes can come out from any part of your body. These techniques will help you overcome phobias, speak with confidence in front of a large congregation, reduce anxiety, and learn how to be in a healthy personal relationship.

Brain Training Success Techniques

Avoid using weak words, such as try. The type of language you will use in your business matters, and you should avoid using vague language. "I will try to get that book tomorrow"—this sentence is not exactly whether you will do it or not. In a business, make your intentions clear, and avoid giving your clients unclear expectations. When dealing with your clients, only use action-based and positive language.

Away from or Move Toward

We all experience problems and obstacles as we move toward success. The way you tackle those problems matters. If you use NLP techniques, it becomes easier. Entrepreneurs have a way of solving their problems. They tend to break tasks, and then they apply logic to it. Then they look at it objectively by removing emotions from that particular problem. You are supposed to move toward the positive "I am capable of doing this. Although it is a difficult job, it is worth it.' And get away from negativity: "This is impossible. I am not able to do this difficult job."

Direction and Focus

NLP helps you use personality to create focus and direction from both a personal and professional perspective, perfect for direct reports in a coaching setting. It involves having an overview of different areas of both life and work, and this helps you have priorities and identify areas of neglect or drift. It enables us to agree to measurable objectives and actions, sharing benefits to both the individual and the organization.

Improving Personal Effectiveness

Improving personal effectiveness is effective in changing the long-term behavior of a person in the workplace. When employees understand one another, it becomes much easier to respond to one another's and the clients' desires and needs. It has been proven that well-functioning and healthy relationships are essential for success in one's personal life.

In conclusion, applying NLP techniques in your business will make you more successful. It is one of the exciting approaches to your problem, and it is worth trying. It improves your way of thinking and helps you achieve your goals.

How to Use NLP to Gain More Wealth and Get Better Results

It is every human being's wish to gain wealth and receive better results in life. We have different ways of doing so, and by using NLP techniques, it is possible to achieve that. These techniques help you to realize yourself and also the best way you can improve your earnings. Those ways are below.

One Can Make Money Using NLP, Using Various Methods

You Can Make Money with NLP as a Coach

Being a coach has many benefits. One can work from anywhere, work at their time, and work at their pay and price. Coaches help clients integrate their desired outcomes, set timelines and deadlines. Create goals, make them achievable, give advice, make the client see things that they cannot see by themselves, and help them stay accountable for what happens to follow up on what is happening.

One Can Also Make Money with NLP as a Practitioner

NLP gives you a tool to work well with people and almost everything that might be bothering them. It has been discovered that most people are looking for NLP practitioners, and one is very marketable. Being a practitioner helps people to:

- **Conquer fear and phobias**

They have different ways of helping people to overcome fear. Sometimes they expose their clients to what they fear most but in a safe and controlled environment. You will realize that you will learn how to combat your anxiety and fear, and after some time, you will be able to control it. Another way they use is teaching their clients the relaxation technique, which will help control both mental and physical feelings of fear. Some practitioners will suggest you seek medical help if you want to treat phobias, and after taking medication, that phobia will go away. Now you can live in everyday life.

- **Lose excess weight**

They usually suggest methods for us to lose weight. These methods include exercising and always practicing healthy diet habits. You are very aware that if you have too much weight, it can lead to you getting diabetes, affecting your everyday life.

- **Quit bad habits**

Habit is defined as a pattern of behaviors acquired through repetition. We have two categories of habits: good and bad habits. These bad habits make us not live a normal life, and this affects our productivity in life. These bad habits include smoking, gambling, etc. Smoking affects our life as nicotine found in cigarettes makes us addicts, and thus, for your body to operate normally, you have to smoke. There are several ways we can break these habits, but it varies from one person to another. It is broken using the following tips:

- **Identify the trigger.** It is the first step when you want to break the habit. Triggers include those things that go through your mind at that exact time. For example, reflect on what always goes through your mind when you are biting your nails.

- **Then try to replace bad behavior with a healthy one.** For instance, if you want to counteract smoking, try to find a new hobby you can practice during free time.

- **Avoid temptations.** Sometimes habits may be linked to a particular place or people. To break the habit, you have to avoid those friends, for instance, who are always drinking or gambling. That way, you can break the bad habit of drinking alcohol.

- **Keep your focus.** When you want to break a bad habit, you have to stay focused and committed to that. You should keep in mind that you are cutting the bad habit for your good. For instance, when quitting smoking, you are supposed to know that you are doing that to avoid getting diseases like cancer.

- **Never lose hope.** Hope is a pillar that keeps us moving. You should consider that you will face many obstacles when you are trying to leave a habit. Thus, you should have a plan to counter that if it arises. Do it once per day, and never give up.

- **Reward yourself.** When you stay away from a bad habit even one day, treat yourself. You buy yourself a new outfit, or you take a vacation. It will motivate you to keep avoiding the bad habit even though you are the one rewarding yourself.

- **Enhance confidence.** Sometimes we face situations that help us become confident. For instance, when you are having a staff meeting, confidence should be displayed. Practitioners help us boost our confidence by assisting us in identifying our weak points and strong points.

Here, people tend to confuse this with being a coach. A coach is different from a consultant in that a coach doesn't tell people what to do but helps clients find answers to their questions while consultants give specialized advice. For example, a business consultant helps his clients with concrete advice on how to grow their businesses.

You can also make money with NLP as an author. NLP training incorporates accelerated learning, NLP subconscious teaching principles, and layered learning. Becoming a published author increases one's credibility in the field, which will allow you to charge expensively.

You can also make money with NLP as a speaker. It again points to the knowledge one would have acquired from NLP. Suppose one continues with training beyond being a practitioner. In that case, they have the chance to enter a Master Trainer Development Program, where they issue all useful materials one requires to become a good speaker.

Chapter 10. Body Language and Behavior Imitation

Our non-verbal, or body language, is one of the most powerful communication methods we use in our day-to-day experiences. It is the mode of contact that ignites feelings and reactions on our "healthy point." Research has shown that understanding body language improves one's potential to effectively get out of any given situation, whatever one wants.

Have you ever encountered a couple sitting together and got a feeling of exactly how good or bad their friendship was in minutes? Have you ever questioned how you could arrive so quickly at this point without any prior interaction? Whether you are aware of it or not, we spend our days listening to people's non-verbal signals interpreted by their body language and drawing conclusions from our assumptions about them.

The body language shows that we conceal from the world in words and how we feel about ourselves, our relationships, and our circumstances. The individuals we associate with will evaluate our motives. The strength of our interactions, how masterful we are in any particular situation, our level of trust, and our real goals and aspirations by our eye contact, movements, body posture, and facial expressions.

The strength of body language is seen in the resulting emotional reaction. In nearly any case, emotions influence choices and reactions. Non-verbal signals activate emotions that define an individual's core properties, such as truthfulness, trustworthiness, honesty, competence level, and willingness to lead.

Understanding these signals will decide who we are going to meet, the work we are being recruited for, the amount of recognition we are having, and even those elected to powerful political positions.

Why do we not spend years studying and improving successful body language skills for such an immense skill? The fact is that most people undervalue the meaning of body language before they try a better interpretation of human conduct in an intimate relationship or in a competitive market situation to achieve an advantage.

Mastery in body language contains the keys for individuals to perceive the context of particular movements and body expressions and understand how to convey and express signals while communicating with others properly. As a result, there is a significant improvement in the general success of public interactions. The easiest way to continue this learning cycle is to study the simple understanding of the two core body language styles—open presence and closed presence.

The closed presence's body language form is illustrated in individuals who fold their bodies around the body's centerline, which runs straight down the middle of the body from the top of the head to the foot. The physical features that produce this form of appearance are feet positioned beside each other, arms held tight to the chest, hands folded across the chest, slight hand movements kept close to the body, shoulders rolling forward, and eyes fixed below eye level.

The world's signals transmitted by the body language form of closed appearance were a loss of confidence, low self-esteem, impotence, and lack of experience. In extreme cases, the message of needing to be invisible may also be produced. The consequences of this kind of body language on the person expressing can range from actually not having the best possible opportunity to a worst-case situation of harboring a self-fulfilling image of victimization.

By comparison, the accessible appearance is displayed in individuals that build a sense of dominance, control, and leadership by projecting mastery of confidence, achievement, energy, and ability. The physical features include feet held hip apart, freehand movements used in speech away from the body's middle line, elbows held away from the chest, shoulders pulled back, upright postures, and eyes fixed on their listeners' eye level. Such people are viewed as desirable, competent, intellectual, and are quickly seen as achieving success. We consider this form of body language as the "leaders' body language."

The aim is eye contact to enhance body language and to start expressing a transparent appearance. Face contact is one of the social devices that we enjoy most. Someone will alter the way others see them by making direct eye contact while communicating with others. Once people start looking straight into a victim's eyes, they are perceived as confident, trustworthy, and professional.

Hand gestures and facial expressions are the second degrees of improvement that one can create for a transparent face to be seen. Both methods of communicating improve the ability to and accurately convey information. Through skillfully using open hand motions away from the body and expressive facial expression, greater emphasis is produced when communicating through engaging the audience more physically and increasing the amount of knowledge provided during the conversation.

Body language mastery is essential to creating the most powerful presence in all human relationships. Individuals lacking this knowledge are vulnerable to confusion and find their attempts inadequate in expressing their thoughts. With the ability to distinguish between the various body language styles, everybody will achieve the competence required to excel in whatever pursuit they want.

Know and Understand Your Body Language

If you know it or not, body language is a significant force responsible for how everyone you encounter comes up with an opinion on you. Listening skills are a must and very necessary in many careers—particularly in careers where you support others to build positive relationships with clients. Whether you help people maintain their relationships, give people advice for business success or educate people about some other form of issue, they see your body language; displaying strong listening skills makes people feel relaxed.

Poor body language could result in something big being lost in you. It doesn't matter to you! Attentively and sincerely listen to every single word. It is the body language that makes you feel necessary to you and gives them the support they need. Understanding what the signs of a lousy listener are here is significant, and you will seek to rid yourself of all of these. When you have the habit of having your arms crossed around your stomach, whether you tap your feet impatiently, move whether turn and look away too much, or while listening, you tell the other person you're not interested in what he or she does. It will most likely lead to the termination of the partnership, which may cause significant business losses.

Ok, what would you do to continue transmitting constructive messages through your body language to the person you're talking to? You will first try to face the other party squarely on. Look not out to give a constructive signal. So at the moment of contact, we fall into the body's posture. You will take a transparent approach. You never have to leave your arms or legs folded; otherwise, the other guy would think you're not interested in listening to his point.

When you lean over when you speak to someone, your body language suggests you pay more attention to what he or she does. Leaning forward, by comparison, suggests you have little confidence whatsoever. The most pivotal aspect is eye touch. Seek to keep eye contact at all times. When you are looking down or turning down, it shows you have no interest in the topic and feel embarrassed.

However, the importance of a confident stance cannot be overlooked either. You don't want to be too uptight. You need not be too formal when talking to anyone, either. When you believe you have experienced significant defeats in the past due to your bad body language, you can instantly start following the above tips.

Behavior Imitation

Behavior imitation is something that can be used for good and for bad. Often, as children, we mimic the behavior of the people around us. It helps us to learn social norms. Also, it helps us feel like we fit into the crowd. Many traditions have been built off of people mimicking other people's behavior.

As we continue to grow up, we continue to imitate the people around us. Here again, it makes us feel as if we belong. Also, it can help us build relationships and understand the people around us more easily. While many people use behavior imitation for the right reasons, many others don't.

Criminals who are socially awkward tend to act like the people around them. It can make it harder to discern the good guys from the bad guys. It is a manipulation tactic that works quite well when people don't know how to behave appropriately. While some people are very good at mimicking those around them, it will be obvious when others try to do this. Cases of extreme social awkwardness will not allow the person to behave like those around them genuinely. It can be a tip to seeing what they may have planned after.

Another way that behavior imitation is prevalent with criminals is when they idolize someone or something. They will change their very persona to reflect that of which they admire. An excellent example of this is people that still follow the ideals of Adolf Hitler. The new generation of Nazis mimics the ways of old because they still believe his blasphemous thoughts to be true. It is truly scary behavior imitation.

Chapter 11. Using NLP to Manage People

When it comes to managing people effectively, it's essential that you first understand the non-verbal cues they provide to apply your skills toward influencing them. It is a necessary principle in using the NLP technique. Following are a few NLP techniques that can allow you to influence people's perception and thinking:

Deciphering Eye Movements

It is essential to realize and know the meaning of eye movements because each eye movement tells its tale. For instance, when searching for the right word or trying to remember a name, you automatically move your eyes in a certain way (most likely, squinting). Rolling the eyes signals contempt or exasperation.

Winking Indicates Flirtation or a Joke

Widening the eyes signals surprise or shock, even extreme excitement. The eyes can reveal much more about people's mental and emotional status, all on their own.

Once you understand what other people's thought processes are, you can accurately follow a course of action or dialogue which acknowledges the unspoken response, as signaled by the eyes. And as you may know, eye movements complement other communication forms such as hand movements, speech, and facial expressions.

Dilation of the pupils, breathing, angle of the body, and the hands' position—all these are complementary to the spoken message. Still, eye movement is essential in communication because every movement is influenced by particular senses and different parts of the brain.

Here is how you can generally interpret eye movement:

Visual Responsiveness

- **Eyes upward, then towards the right:** Whenever a person tilts eyes upward and then to the right, it means that the person is formulating a mental picture.
- **Eyes upward, then towards the left:** Whenever a person tilts eyes upward, followed by an eye movement to the left, it means the person recalls a particular image.
- **Eyes looking straight ahead:** Whenever someone focuses directly in front of them, this indicates that the person is not focused on anything in particular. That is the look often referred to as 'glazed.'

Auditory Responsiveness

- **Eyes looking towards the right:** When a person's eyes shift straight towards the right, it means the person is in the process of constructing a sound.
- **Eyes looking towards the left:** When a person's eyes shift straight towards the left, it indicates that the person recalls a sound.

Audio-Digital Responsiveness

- **Eyes looking downward, then switching to the left:** When someone drops their eyes and then proceeds to turn

their eyes to the left, this signals that the person is engaged in internal dialogue.
- **Eyes looking right down then left to right:** When a person looks down and then proceeds to turn their eyes to the left and then to the right in consecutive movements, it means the person is engaged in negative self-talk.

Kinesthetic Responsiveness

Here, the person looks directly down, only to turn the eyes to the right. That is an indication that the person is evaluating emotional status. It further indicates that the person is not at ease:

- Verbal responses

- Rhythmic speech

The idea here is not to be poetic as you speak, but to speak at a regular pace. The recommended pace of speaking is equated to the heartbeat, say, between 45 and 72 beats per minute. At that pace, you are likely to sustain the listener's attention and establish greater receptivity to what you're saying. While normal conversational speed averages about 140 words per minute, slowing down a little and taking time to pause is highly effective to sustain people's attention. Your regular cadence should be punctuated by fluctuations in tone and emphasis in order not to sound monotonous.

Repeating Key Words

When you try to influence someone, some keywords or phrases carry additional weight as far as your message is concerned. This speaking method is a way of embedding the message in the listener and subtly suggesting that your message is valid and worthy of reception. Repeating key words also suggests commitment, conviction, and mastery of the subject matter.

Using Strongly Suggestive Language

Use a supportive and positive language of what you are saying, using a selection set of strong, descriptive words or phrases. As you do this, you should observe the person you are speaking to closely, in a way that makes them feel as though you see right through them and aware of what they are thinking.

Don't be invasive about this or aggressive. Merely suggest that you have a keen appreciation of what makes people tick by way of your gaze. It places you in a dominant position, especially when accompanied by dominant body language, like "steepling." It helps to use suitable, complementary body language as you speak to underscore the message subtly.

Touching the Person Lightly, As You Speak

Touching the person as you speak to them draws their attention to you in a relaxed and familiar way. By employing this technique, you're preparing the listener to absorb what you say to them, a way of programming attentiveness. Those engaging in inter-gender conversations in the workplace should take great care with this technique, as it can lead to misunderstandings.

Using a Mixture of "Hot" and "Vague" Words

"Hot" words are those that tend to provoke specific sensations in the listener. When you use them to influence someone's thinking, it is advisable to use them in a suitable pattern. Examples of phrases containing hot words are: it means; feel free; see this; because; hear this. The effect of employing these words and phrases is that you're directing influencing the listener's state of mind, including how that person feels, imagines, and perceives.

You're also appealing to the sense most prevalent in the listener's perceptive style (as observed through the movement of their eyes). For example, the phrase "hear this" will appeal to those who indicate a tendency to respond most actively to auditory stimuli.

Using the Interspersal Technique

The interspersal technique states one thing while hoping to impress on the listener something entirely different. For example, you could make a positive statement like:

"John is very generous, but some people take advantage of him and treat him as gullible."

When someone hears this statement, the likely assumption is that you want people to appreciate John's generosity. That is likely to be the message heard, and yet, the subtext is that while John is generous, he is also considered gullible and, thus, at a disadvantage in life when it comes to other people. Your hidden agenda may influence the listener to think of John as gullible, which calls into question his judgment. So, emphasize the words "but" and "gullible."

The word "but" serves to transition the perceived compliment to John to an implicit slight. The techniques just described form strategies in the service of influencing people.

They're not intended to force a viewpoint or to control people's behavior for nefarious ends. These techniques are intended to modify undesirable behaviors, resulting in workplace difficulties, including staff failure to work well together or complete team projects.

They're also accommodating in relationships with young people and children, whether at home or in a learning environment.

Techniques of subtle manipulative effects like those described, though capable of influencing people and their behavior, don't amount to anything even approaching coercion. The person being spoken to chooses all responses and is merely influenced or steered toward those responses.

Conclusion

Now we get how the whole thing works, we're not that fond of it, but we understand the basics. The main question now, though, is how do you guard against it? That's really what we've been trying to figure out this whole time. How do you prevent someone from pulling all that NLP mumbo jumbo on you when you're not looking? This part of the guide is for you because we have a few pointers for you.

Beware of Matchers

The first thing you're going to want to do is to take in and apply everything you've just learned. Remember all that stuff about matching and mirroring? Well, now you need to be on the lookout for it. When you speak to someone you think is trying to control you, make a point to note how they react to your body language. Are they sitting in the same pattern you are? Are they copying your movements as well?

If you're unsure, try testing it out by changing your posture and then wait to see if they mimic it. With pro NLP practitioners, the mimicking may be a bit subtler and a bit more delayed, but the unskilled ones are a total giveaway. They'll copy the posture right away, and automatically, you know what you're up against.

Now that you know, you can either call them out on their behavior or, if you want to have a little fun, start applying NLP on them to confuse them! Not only will you catch them off guard, but if you can pull it off, you can get them to tell you what their whole ploy was all about and who put them up to it. Total win!

Consciously Infuse Randomness in Your Eye Movement

When it comes to confusing your opponent and playing them at their own game, there is little going to give you the same amount of satisfaction as random play. Random eye movements are like going to the gym with your iPod on shuffle. Nobody knows what's coming on after. It's basically like trolling your manipulators in real-time, and it can be quite fun.

Any NLP user worth their salt is going to go in hard with the whole eye movement thing. It is because your eye movements tell them how you assess and store information, which is precisely why some people can tell if you are lying or cheating just by looking at your eyes. When they say your eyes speak volumes, this is what they mean!

So how do you avoid being read by an NLP practitioner? Simple, use random eye movements. As you are speaking, make a point to look left or right or up or down. You can even make a game of it. Left for complex sentences, down for every question, and simple sentences can go right or up, depending on whether they start with a vowel.

Pick Up on Ambiguity

One of the tricks that NLP kind of sneaks in from hypnotherapy is the full use of vague, unclear language. A great example of the use of this technique is Donald Trump's "Make America Great" Again Campaign.

Even though the now-president went around campaigning about making a better version of America, he never really broke down what that meant. It was such a hazy term that it could mean anything to anyone, and that was precisely what he wanted.

Whenever anyone starts using stuff like that on you, such as "release your inner troubles and feel the world move slowly around you in conjunction with your prospective earthly successes." What you're doing is allowing hypnotherapy to program your internal state in a specific form. It helps the other person when they then try to convince you to do something that benefits them.

Anytime you feel that someone is trying to do something like that to you, force yourself to snap out of it and ask specific questions, "What exactly do you mean by 'great'?" or "What potential are you talking about?" Take note; all you have to do is point it out. Once you've done that, you're home free!

Be Hypersensitive to People Permitting You to Do Stuff

The other thing you should watch out for? Permissive language. When a person says something like "you can do XYZ" or "Feel free to make yourself at home" or even something tempting like, "If you want, you can borrow the new Avengers movie from me," what they are doing is preparing you to enter into a trance state. You see, experienced NLP users never outright tell their subjects to do anything. They suggest, recommend, or allow. In this way, the subject feels like they are in control, whereas control was wiped out a long time ago in reality! So then, feel free to say no thanks!

Read Between the Lines

We're onto reading between the lines. You have to keep in mind that people who use or people who are using NLP to control you or to manipulate you tend to use specific controlled langue, and nine out of ten times, you are not going to know what hit you.

How do they do it? Double meanings. And you'll find them in the unexpected places, so skilled NLP users who are good at what they do know how to use double meaning infused sentences to get you to think the way they want you to. Imagine that you are the evil witch's neighbor from the Hansel and Gretel story; now you don't eat kids, but you do have a thing for snacks. Your NLP user, A.K.A "the evil witch" comes up to you and says, "Children make nutritious snacks, just in case you were wondering." Sure the witch claims she was talking about their production capacity, but what you heard and processed was something a little different, and already you're a bit more inclined to take a little nibble.

Be Attentive

You need to be very careful about how much attention you are paying to your surroundings and what's going on in them. We get you that you can't always be super alert, but you need to know that you are vulnerable when you aren't alert. For example, an essential tactic that employers use when negotiating salary packages is waiting until the employee in question seems a little off and then jumping in. Saying that they haven't negotiated a pay difference for Tom, Dick, and Harry and don't foresee a lot of change in the other employees. Not much change at all, they repeat. Automatically, now that you are asked how much change in salary you expect, you say not much change—congratulations! You've just been programmed!

Watch Your Mouth

Another important tip? Watch what you say. Master manipulators tend to create a false sense of urgency to make you feel that you have to do this particular thing by this specific time, or else something drastic will happen. You don't have a choice. You have to do this now! What do you do? Well, nothing. Yes, seriously, nothing. Never make any important decisions at the drop of a hat. Chances are you're not the president of the United States, meaning no nuclear codes lie with you, which of course, means that you don't need to make any immediate decisions without consulting people. You don't have to make any quick decisions at all.

Sit tight. Getting you to commit is a classic dark psychology move to create a sense of obligation after being exploited. Please don't fall for it!

Trust Your Gut

And your final rule, which also happens to be your most important, is to trust your gut. Your instincts know a lot more than you do, mostly because your subconscious mind is processing signs and symbols at a rate your conscious brain can't even begin to fathom. So if it is out there telling you that something is up and that something needs to be done about it, then you need to make sure that you are on your guard ready to get things done because, like a used car salesman, you are more likely than not in the hands of a master practitioner.

www.ingramcontent.com/pod-product-compliance
Lightning Source LLC
Chambersburg PA
CBHW071122030426
42336CB00013BA/2169